I LAUGH THROUGH TEARS

The Ballades of François Villon

Cy comence le grant codicille q̃ te
ſtamēt maiſtre francoꝭ Villon

APOCRYPHAL PORTRAIT OF VILLON
—Villon, *Le Grant Testament*
(1489)

I Laugh through Tears

The Ballades of François Villon

Translated from the French
by
G. P. CUTTINO

PHILOSOPHICAL LIBRARY
New York

For MYRTLE

'En l'an de mon trentiesme aage,
Que toutes mes hontes j'eus beues,
Ne du tout fol, ne du tout sage'
Le Testament, 1-3.

PREFACE

My first essay at translating Villon was provoked by the English rendering of his most famous ballade that finds its way into most anthologies as part of the poetical legacy of Dante Gabriel Rossetti. That was back in the halcyon days of 1938, when I was making the boat trip from Vienna to Budapest. A closer study of the ballades since then has left me wondering how Rossetti, Swinburne, and their ilk could ever have mustered enough courage to produce even their emasculated versions, for Villon spoke in accents considerably more foreign to the ears of our grandfathers than they are to ours. Victorian England and fifteenth-century France were as far apart as were the languages and centuries that separated them.

The path that leads to an understanding and an appreciation of François Villon, whatever may be its beginnings, must inevitably go by way of that incomparable study from the pen of D. B. Wyndham Lewis. The translations that follow are small interest on the heavy debt all Villon lovers owe to this biographer, and quite a few of the lines and many of the notes will bear witness to this debt. The first drafts of the translations were done at Fédhala and Maison Blanche between September 1943 and June 1944, when I was serving in the Army in French North Africa. Several of my fellow officers were very helpful in untangling some of the linguistic problems, and to them I am very grateful. During the past several months I have completed the final revisions, profiting from the excellent criticisms and welcome encouragement of my friends, Townsend Scudder III and Edward Weismiller.

Working from Lucien Foulet's fourth revision of the *Oeuvres*, edited by Auguste Longnon, I have attempted above all to make the translations as literal as the English language and the stiff ballade form permit. All the ballades are here, except those of the *Jargon*, which I leave to others more learned than I in the mystifying argot of fifteenth-century Paris. I trust Villon speaks for himself, that I have steered clear of the stained glass and the flamboyance of the pseudo-Gothics.

G.P.C.

CONTENTS

INTRODUCTION

François de Montcorbier et des Loges was born in Paris in 1431/2, during the English occupation of the city. About 1438 he went to live with a distant relative, Master Guillaume de Villon, resident chaplain of the University Church of Saint-Benoît-le-Bientourné, and assumed his guardian's name. It was about 1443 when Villon entered the University of Paris, where he won his bachelor's degree in the Faculty of Arts in March 1449 and his Licentiate and Master of Arts between 4 May and 26 August 1452. He undoubtedly participated in the student riots that took place in 1451-52 over the moving of a stone known as the Pet-au-Deable.

His first real brush with the forces of law and order, however, occurred on 5 June 1455, when Philippe Chermoye, a priest, was killed in a fight, presumably over a wench called Ysabeau, in the cloister of Saint-Benoît. Villon found it expedient to quit Paris. He spent his time in Bourg-la-Reine, about eight kilometres away. Obtaining letters of remission from Charles VII in the matter of the death of Chermoye, Villon returned to Paris in January 1456 and wrote *Le Lais*.

On Christmas Eve of the same year, 500 *écus d'or* were stolen from the College of Navarre. Again Villon left Paris. For four years he wandered to the south and west of the city. Bourg-la-Reine, Angers, Bourges, and Saint-Génerou are named in his poetry as places where he spent some of his time. He celebrated the birth of Princess Marie d'Orléans at Blois on 19 December 1457, participating in the poetical activities of the court of her father, Duke Charles. On or shortly after 17 July 1460, he was saved from hanging by the entry of the same Princess into Orléans. A little more than a year later, on 2 October 1461, Villon was languishing in the prison of Thibault d'Assigny, bishop of Orléans, at Meung-sur-Loire. Tradition has it that he had lifted a votive lamp from a church near Baccon-sur-Loire. At any rate, this time he was saved by a royal progress of Louis XI through the town. Thence he went to Moulins, after having touched John, duke of Bourbon, for a loan.

Early in 1462 Villon composed his masterpiece, *Le Testament,* inserting in it numerous ballades that belong to earlier years. Returning to Paris, he was jailed in the Châtelet during 3-7 November for a minor theft. The Faculty of Theology of the University, having a long memory in such matters, obtained his release after requiring him to sign a bond promising restitution of 120 *écus d'or* of the haul taken from the College of Navarre. Scarcely had the ink dried on this document when he became implicated in the death of a papal notary, Master François Ferrebourg, murdered during a drunken brawl. This time the authorities were not so lenient: he was thrown in the Châtelet and sentenced to be 'hanged and strangled'. But Villon's luck still held. Parlement, on his appeal, commuted the death sentence to banishment for ten years. This was on 5 January 1463; after this date, Villon disappears from history. To the period after this time belong the stories of Rabelais that have him ending his days as court poet to Edward V of England and in a retreat at Saint-Maixent in Poitou. Authorities place the date of his death about 1489.

The ballade, as its etymology suggests (Provençal *ballada* from the Latin *ballare,* to dance), was originally a dancing song. A form of verse invented by the Arabs, it came to southern France by way of Spain and Italy. The troubadours took it up and passed it on to the trouvères, their counterparts of the *langue d'oïl.* In its old form, the ballade consisted of three couplets, or stanzas, of the same number of feet and of the same length, having the same rhymes, some masculine, the others feminine, and ending with the same line as a refrain. The three couplets were followed by a fourth and shorter one, ending with the common refrain and called the *envoi,* usually beginning with the word *Prince.* The ballade was *redoublée* when the refrain consisted of two lines, placed either consecutively or one in the middle and the other at the end of the stanza. The characteristic qualities of the early ballades were simplicity, naïveté, naturalness, and grace.

Villon employed in all seventeen different rhyme schemes in his ballades. The most common is the ballade of three stanzas, each rhymed *ababbcbC* with an envoy rhymed *bcbC*, capitals representing the refrain. This is the simplest, and perhaps the most effective, form, and it is used in thirteen of the ballades (1-4, 7-9, 12, 14-16, 19, 30). The other schemes are as follows: six stanzas of *ababbcbC,* envoy lacking (ballade 5); three stanzas of *ababbccdcD,* envoy *cccdccD* (ballades 6, 13); three stanzas of *ababbccdcD,* envoy *ccdcD* (ballade 10); three stanzas of *ababbbbcbC,* envoy *bcbC* (ballade 11); three stanzas of *ababbccdcD,* envoy *ccddccD* (ballade 17); four stanzas of *ababbcbC,* envoy *bcbC* (ballade 18); three stanzas of *ababbcbC,* envoy *bbbcbC* (ballade 20); three stanzas of *ababccddedE,* envoy *ddedE* (ballade 21); three stanzas of *ababbccdcD,* envoy *ccdcD* (ballades 22, 25, 29); six stanzas of *ababbcbC,* envoy *bcbC* (ballade 23); three stanzas of *ababbccdcD,* envoy *ccdccD* (ballade 24); three stanzas of *ababbccddedE,* envoy *ddedE* (ballade 27); three stanzas of *ababbbbcbC,* envoy *bbcbC* ballade 28); four stanzas of *ababbccdcD,* envoy *cccdccD* (ballade 26); three stanzas of *ababbccddedE,* envoy *dedE* (ballade 31); three stanzas of *ababbaacAC,* envoy lacking (ballade 32). Only the last is a true *ballade redoublée.*

Ignoring the variations in numbers of stanzas and in the pattern of the envoys, the basic rhyme schemes are:

> *a b a b b c b C* (17 ballades)
> *a b a b b c c d c D* (9 ballades)
> *a b a b b b b c b C* (2 ballades)
> *a b a b b c c d d e d E* (2 ballades)
> *a b a b c c d d e d E* (1 ballade)
> *a b a b b a a c A C* (1 ballade)

There are, then, at the most only five rhymes in a ballade, and the majority of ballades have only three. For this reason, and owing to the scarcity of appropriate rhymes in English, it is impossible, when translating, to retain the rhyme scheme of the original. The most that can be done is to keep the refrain throughout and to follow the original rhyme within each stanza rather than throughout the entire ballade.

The ballades are written in octameter (15) and decameter (17). They are here translated into tetrameter, which sets a pace more akin to that of the original than does the customary pentameter.

How far Villon has got away from the naïve simplicity of earlier ballades the reader will be able to judge for himself.

From LE TESTAMENT

JOAN OF ARC
—*Le Rozier historial de France*
(1523)

BALLADE OF LADIES OF OTHER YEARS

Dictes moy ou, n'en quel pays

Pray tell me where, beyond what seas
Is Roman Flora, fair of face,
Thaïs or Alcibiades,
Of equal lineage, equal grace;
And Echo leading endless chase
Above the river and the mere,
Whose beauty bore no mortal trace?
Where are the snows of yesteryear?

Where is the learned Héloïse,
Whose love brought Peter Abelard
A eunuch's penance on his knees
At Saint-Denis in a cloistered yard;
Where is the queen with soul so hard
That Buridan, sackbound, should steer
A course down the Seine in wet discard?
Where are the snows of yesteryear?

Queen Blanche as white as fleur-de-lys
Who sang a siren's muted strain,
Bietris, big-foot Berthe, Alis,
And Arembour who held the Maine,
And Joan the good who quit Lorraine,
Burnt at Rouen on an English bier,
Mother of God, where are they lain?
Where are the snows of yesteryear?

Envoy

O Prince, seek not to know this week
Where they may be, or yet this year,
While this refrain returns to speak:
Where are the snows of yesteryear?

Flora is the celebrated Roman courtesan mentioned by Juvenal,
Satires, ii. 9. *Thaïs* will be familiar to those who know the works of

Massenet and Anatole France. *Alcibiades* is probably to be identified with the name Boethius cites in praise of heroic beauty. Villon, who was never too attentive at lectures, probably caught the name indistinctly. *Héloïse* and *Abelard* are too well known for further comment to be necessary. The site of their house is presumed to be at 9, Quai aux Fleurs. There is no historical foundation for the *Buridan* legend. He was a celebrated professor of the University of Paris and a disciple of William of Ockham. The Queen may be Marguerite of Burgundy, adulterous wife of Louis X le Hutin (1314-16). She lived in a tower on the site of the west pavilion of the Palais Mazarin, where she made it her practice to entice any passers-by who took her fancy. When satisfied, she had her lovers thrown in the Seine. Somewhat like the victims of the defenestration at Prague, Buridan escaped by falling on a straw-laden barge, towed under the tower by his students. *Queen Blanche* may be Blanche of Castile, mother of Louis IX le Saint. *Big-foot Berthe* was the wife of Pepin le Bref, and in the legends, mother of Charlemagne. *Bietris* was the wife, of Hervi de Metz, in the chanson de geste of that name. *Arembour* was the wife of Foulque V, count of Anjou. *Joan,* of course, is Saint Joan of Arc.

BALLADE OF LORDS OF OTHER YEARS

Qui plus, ou est le tiers Calixte

Where is Calixtus III, the great
And last departed of that name,
Who four years sat in papal state?
And Aragonese Alfonso's fame,
And gracious Bourbon? What became
Of Breton Arthur's ducal strain
And Charles whom none could ever blame?
But where is valiant Charlemagne?

Likewise where is the Scottish king
Whose face from brow to chin, they say,
Was like an amethyst, a thing
Vermilion to his dying day?
The king in Cyprus holding sway,
Alas! and that good king of Spain
Whose name I cannot call today?
But where is valiant Charlemagne?

From speaking further I desist;
The world is all derision.
He lives not who can death resist
Or find therein provision.
A further question I require:
Bohemia felt László's reign—
Where is he now? Where is his sire?
But where is valiant Charlemagne?

Envoy

Where is Du Guesclin, can you tell?
The Dauphin of Auvergne's domain
And Alençon's proud duke as well?
But where is valiant Charlemagne?

Calixtus III (Alfonso Borgia) was pope for three years and four
months. He died in 1458. It was he who appointed the ecclesiastical

commission charged with reviewing the trial of Joan of Arc. *Alfonso V*, called the Wise or the Magnanimous, was king of Aragon. He conquered Naples and died there on 28 June 1458. *Arthur III* of Brittany, who died in the same year, was count of Richemont and constable of France. He distinguished himself in the final battles of the 100 Years War. Charles I, *duke of Bourbon*, and uncle of Charles VI of France, died in 1456. He was one of the most cultured men of his age. *Charles VII* (1422-61), a contemporary of Henry VI of England, was the king whose surname was changed from the Indolent to the Victorious, largely through the efforts of Joan of Arc. The *Scottish king* is James II, who supported Charles VII against the English and took the part of the House of York during the Wars of the Roses. He died on 3 August 1460 as the result of an accident during the siege of Roxburgh. The *king of Spain* so easily forgotten is doubtless Juan II of Castile (died 1458), father of the more famous Isabella. *László* (Lancelot) of Austria, king of Bohemia, died in 1457. Bertrand *du Guesclin* (Claquin), once held by the Black Prince for a ransom of 100,000 *doubles d'or*, finally ended by chasing the English from Normandy, Gascony, Saintonge, Poitou, and Limousin. He was the most famous French general of the 100 Years War. He died at the siege of Châteauneuf-de-Random in 1380. The *dauphin of Auvergne* (died 1426) is Béraud II. The *duke of Alençon* is most likely Jean IV, killed at Agincourt in 1415. In the Envoy, Villon refers to the preceding generation, while the remainder of the ballade is concerned with men who have just died.

BALLADE IN OLD FRENCH

Car, ou soit ly sains apostolles

Where is the apostolic pope
With alb and amice clothed and crowned,
Whose holy stole had strength to rope
Mephistophelian neck around,
All hot with evil, choked and bound?
His minions perished in his day,
Dead leaves of life upon the ground:
The wind has whisked them all away.

And he who filled Byzantium's throne,
The emperor with fist of gold,
Or France's very noble own,
More famed than all the kings of old,
Who for a love of God untold
Built churches that a land might pray;
His age brought honours manifold.
The wind has whisked them all away.

The dauphin of Grenoble's spires,
And Viénne's proud and valiant soul;
Where are the elder sons and sires
Of Salins, Dijon, and of Dole,
Their liveried servants' measured stroll,
Pursuivants, heralds, buglers gay,
With noses reddened at the bowl?
The wind has whisked them all away.

Envoy

Princes are destined all to die
And others are but living clay;
What matters their protesting cry?
The wind has whisked them all away.

France's 'very noble own' is undoubtedly Louis IX le Saint (1226-70).
The references to the dauphins of *Viennois,* to the dukes and counts of
Burgundy, who were lords of *Salins, Dijon,* and *Dole,* are apparently
to no particular individuals.

THE PRICE OF LOVE
—*Les Demandes d'amour avec les reponses*
(ca. 1504)

LA BELLE HEAULMIÈRE TO THE DAUGHTERS OF JOY

Or y pensez, belle Gantiere

'My pretty Glover, think on this,
Apprenticed to me until late,
And Blanche the Cobbler, never miss,
For now you must consolidate.
Take right and left and do not wait;
I beg you, spare no man, but haste:
For agèd trulls are tarnished plate,
Like money clipped and then debased.

'And you who stuff the sausage skins,
Adept at dancing—this the least—
And Guillemette with all your pins,
Never forget your man's a beast:
The shutters close when trade has ceased;
And you'll be old and flaked like paste,
Fit but to serve a toothless priest,
Like money clipped and then debased.

'Jehanneton with all your hoods,
Beware the pox within you sown;
And Katherine with spurs and goods,
Relent before your birds are flown:
An ugly strumpet holds her own
By laughing down a man's distaste.
Love always scorns an aging crone,
Like money clipped and then debased.

Envoy
'So, girls, best cock a heeding ear
To that with which I now am faced:
No longer current—that is clear,
Like money clipped and then debased.'

The wife of the helmet maker, in the full bloom of her beauty in 1415, at the time this ballade was composed was relegated to the position of mistress to Nicolas d'Orgement, archdeacon of Paris. The other names mentioned are obviously those of ladies who shared her profession.

DOUBLE BALLADE

Pour ce, amez tant que vouldrez

Then love until you have your fill,
Follow the ball and midnight feast,
The end will bring you naught until
You break your head, to say the least;
For foolish loves make man a beast:
Idolatrous was Solomon,
And thereby Samson's vision ceased.
Happier those who all this shun!

And Orpheus, sweet troubadour,
Who piped his flute among the dead,
Risked mortal peril on its spoor
From Cerberus of the triple head;
And beautiful Narcissus fled,
Because of love too lightly won,
To seek his peace in a watery bed.
Happier those who all this shun!

Sardana, once a valiant knight,
Who conquered all the realm of Crete,
Aped woman's form and took delight
In girlish chores and things effete;
And David, quitting wisdom's seat,
Forgot his fear of God for one
Whose perfumed thighs aroused his heat.
Happier those who all this shun!

And Amnon, drunk with carnal power,
Feigning to gorge himself the while,
Plucked lovely Tamar's virgin flower,
A deed incestuous and vile;
Herod—and here I use no guile—
Had John the Baptist's head undone
For a dance, a song, a dancer's smile.
Happier those who all this shun!

Of my poor self I wish to speak:
Beaten like washing in a stream,
Entirely nude—no tongue in cheek—
Who made me chew such sour cream
But Kate Vausselles? Noël I deem
Made up the three to share the fun.
Such wedding mittens costly seem.
Happier those who all this shun!

But is this hot, young blood to spurn
Their tender love and flee their sight?
May God forbid! Such ought to burn
As witches do who ride the night.
Sweeter than civets their delight,
But not to put your trust upon:
For be they brown or be they white,
Happier those who all this shun!

The biblical and mythological characters are familiar enough, but Villon's mythology is somewhat askew. In the original, Cerberus, for the sake of metre, is given one more head than he had a right to. Narcissus died from a surfeit of his own beauty, not from love of a woman. Villon very likely picked up this error from the *Roman de la Rose*. *Sardana* may be Sardanapalus or Saladin, or the name may come from Villon's own mind or be borrowed from some forgotten romance. *Kate Vausselles*, an enigmatic figure, was the torment and obsession of Villon's life. She had him whipped by *Noël le Jolis*. The mention of wedding mittens refers to an old country custom. After the marriage ceremony, guests would remove their gloves and playfully beat one another, saying, 'Remember this wedding!'

BALLADE AS A PRAYER TO OUR LADY

Dame du ciel, regente terrienne

Lady of heaven, earthly queen,
Empress even of Satan's sect,
Receive me now, thy Christian mean,
And count me one with thine elect,
Though I deserve but small respect.
The favours thou dost sweet impart
Lie heavy on my sinful heart;
Without them souls would vainly try
To enter heaven. For my part,
In this faith would I live and die.

Say to thy Son I beg His care;
By Him be all my sins erased;
Like Mary hear my humble prayer,
Or like Theophilus abased,
By Thee absolved and rendered chaste,
Despite the league he made with hell—
Preserve me from its clutches fell,
O Virgin bearing ever high
The mass's sacramental spell:
In this faith would I live and die.

I am a woman poor and old
Who nothing knows, nor letter read.
Within thy parish minster's fold
The painted harps and lutes are spread
Above the damned and boiling dead:
One dreadful scene, one joyful sight
That cover me, Divine Delight
To whom all sinners soon draw nigh,
With boundless faith beyond respite:
In this faith would I live and die.

Envoy

O worthy Virgin, thou who bore
Jesus Who reigns forevermore
Omnipotent—from trials sore
To succour us He came on high
And by His blood our souls restore—
Through thee our Saviour I implore:
In this faith would I live and die.

This ballade is put into the mouth of Villon's mother. She was a native of Anjou. *Mary* is Saint Mary of Egypt, the penitent whose story is told in *The Golden Legend. Theophilus* was vidame of the church of Adana in Galicia. He is a familiar figure in medieval history and finds a place in the tympanum of the north cloister door of Notre Dame de Paris. Best guess as to the church referred to is that it was the Church of the Celestines near the Bastille. It was dedicated to the Annunciation and was particularly celebrated for its wall paintings of heaven and hell. Rabelais died in this quarter of Paris. Villon's mother was still living in 1461, at the time this ballade was written. The Envoy carries his acrostic.

BALLADE TO HIS LOVE

Faulse beauté qui tant me couste chier

False beauty who have cost me dear,
Hypocrisy as sweet as sin,
Love harder to the mouth, I fear,
Than steel, to my destruction kin,
Felon who charm to death within,
O pride on pity never fed,
Can ever scornful eyes begin
To save this wretch whose hope has fled?

Much better were it had I sought
Another's help, to salve my pride;
Then nothing could such pain have brought.
I now must flee and shameful hide.
The great, the lesser side by side!
Haro! Without a blow I'm dead?
Will she through pity turn aside
To save this wretch whose hope has fled?

A time will see your flower fade,
And yellowed, lose its fairest hue;
Then I should laugh, if it but paid;
But only fools will take their due:
For I'll be wrinkled, old as you;
Drink deep before the springs are bled.
And spare from all this pain a few
To save this wretch whose hope has fled.

Envoy

Amorous prince, the gage of love,
Set not your curse upon my head;
But ought you not, for Him above,
To save this wretch whose hope has fled?

The acrostic **MARTHE** in the second stanza of the original apparently refers to the lady who caught Villon on the rebound after his bitter experience with Kathérine de Vausselles.

BALLADE AND PRAYER

Pere Noé, qui plantastes la vigne

Father Noah, who sowed the vine,
You also, Lot, who drank until
Desire, that strong and heady wine,
Aroused your daughters to their fill
(I do not mean to utter ill),
Chief Steward, learned in this art,
Receive, if such may be your will,
The soul of Master John Cotart!

A man of your own lineage bred,
Who drank the dearest and the best,
Though never worth a groat of lead;
But none could at his bowing jest;
Nor from his hands the bottle wrest;
To drinking well he gave his heart.
O noble sirs, then put to rest
The soul of Master John Cotart!

To bed with staggered, reeling gait
I've often seen him pick his way,
And once he even banged his pate
On a butcher's stall, as I can say;
In short, you'll find for night or day
No better tosspot at the part.
Then let him in when you hear bray
The soul of Master John Cotart!

Envoy

O Prince, with mouth too dry to spit
He always roared: 'My tonsils smart!'
And never could his thirst be quit—
The soul of Master John Cotart.

Jehan Cotart was a lawyer of the court of the diocese of Paris, bearing the title of Proctor. He died in 1461. The *Chief Steward* is he of the wedding feast of Cana in Galilee. The others are familiar.

BALLADE FOR ROBERT D'ESTOUTEVILLE

Au poinct du jour, que l'esprevier s'esbat

At daybreak when the falcon wings
To moult and preen his noble dress,
And when the joyous mavis sings
To greet his mate in sweet caress,
What sharp desires upon me press
To grant what lovers may contend!
Know Love has written nothing less;
And we are pledged unto this end.

You'll be the lady of my heart
Without debate, until I die,
A laurel wreath to fight my part
Or olive for each bitter sigh.
Reason compels me now to try,
And to her argument I bend,
To serve you with a binding tie;
And we are pledged unto this end.

What's more, when grief has struck me down,
To Fortune all too often known,
Your sweet eye turns her evil frown
As feathers by the wind are blown.
If you lose not the seed I've sown,
Your field will bear a fruitful blend.
God bade me fill you with my own;
And we are pledged unto this end.

Envoy

Princess, now hear what I declare:
My heart forever will depend
Upon your heart; I hold you there;
And we are pledged unto this end.

The bond between Villon and Robert d'Estouteville, provost of Paris,
is one of those curious alliances between disreputable brilliancy and

eminent respectability. It may be that the two met in Saumur in 1446, where Estouteville won his bride, Ambroise de Loré (to whom the ballade is addressed, as the acrostic in the original shows), daughter of the Baron d'Ivry, in single combat with the Sire de Beauvais. At any rate, the friendship proved highly valuable to Villon, particularly in scrapes like the Pet-au-Deable riots in 1451-52.

BALLADE

En realgar, en arcenic rochier

In arsenic, sulphurous red,
Saltpetre, orpiment, and lime,
To round them off, in boiling lead,
Tempered in lye and resinous grime
Of Jewish piss and fecal slime,
In washings from a leprous chyle,
In scrapings got from every stile,
In aspic's blood, with poison tried,
In badgers', wolves', and foxes' bile,
Let all these envious tongues be fried!

In brain of a cat who hates to fish,
So black, so old, no tooth in head,
In froth and foam—an equal dish—
Of an aging mastiff seeing red,
In scum by a blown-out donkey bred,
Cut into bits by a scissor blade,
In water where the rats have played,
Toads, frogs, and beasts on every side,
Where serpents, lizards, birds have stayed,
Let all these envious tongues be fried!

In mercury that's death to try,
In an adder's navel, never clean,
In blood that barbers leave to dry
On pallets when the full moon's seen,
One black, the other chivish green,
In chancre, scabs, in golden tub
Where nurses soak their rags and rub,
In bidets harlots keep inside
(Known only in a bawdy pub),
Let all these envious tongues be fried!

Envoy

O Prince, strain all these bits divine,
If sacks and sieves are not your line,
Through pants whose seats are stained and dyed;
But first, in droppings from the swine
Let all these envious tongues be fried!

It is supposed that this ballade is aimed at one François Perdrier. Villon had got into difficulty in Bourges around 1458, probably something having to do with blasphemy or heresy, was hailed before the bishop's court, where he met Perdrier, one of his old cronies. Instead of coming to his assistance, Perdrier denounced him.

THE CONTREDITS OF FRANC GONTIER

Sur mol duvet assis, ung gras chanoine

On a downy couch a canon sat,
A brazier warmed his cozy bay,
Dame Sidoine lolled against his fat—
White, tender, sweet, and very gay—
Drinking hippocras night and day;
They laugh and pet and kiss and toy.
I saw them stripped for easy joy
Through a mortise hole upon my knees:
And then I knew, against annoy
There's treasure but to live at ease.

Had Helen and Franc Gontier
But followed this voluptuous trail,
Shallots that take your breath away
Would not outlast a sudden gale.
All of their curds and filthy kale
Aren't worth a pip—I tell it straight.
If of a rosebush couch they prate,
Are feather beds preferred to trees?
What say you? Need you hesitate?
There's treasure but to live at ease.

They munch on oats and barley-bun,
Drink water all the livelong year.
Not all the birds from Babylon
Could cozen my discerning ear
For a single day with life so drear.
For God's sake, let them sigh and pine
Beneath their pretty eglantine:
What's it to me if such things please;
Though rustic life's an anodyne,
There's treasure but to live at ease.

Envoy

Prince, judge that we may all agree.
And though I care not to displease,
Still, as a child they cautioned me:
There's treasure but to live at ease.

This is Villon's own reply to an artificial pastoral, *Les Dictz de Franc Gontier,* which had been published a century before by Philippe de Vitry, later bishop of Meaux.

BALLADE OF THE LADIES OF PARIS

Quoy qu'on tient belles langagieres

As talkers some may well esteem
Venetian wench or Florentine,
At least to hatch a shady scheme,
And even those of classic mien;
Romans and Lombards I have seen
And Genevese, but all the same,
Savoyard or a Piedmont queen,
There's none can touch the Paris dame.

For pretty speech they hold a chair,
The Neapolitans, some say;
And mark you well for cackling fair
The German and the Prussian way;
Though Greeks and though Egyptians may
With Magyars share a lisping fame
Or Spaniards or Castilians gay,
There's none can touch the Paris dame.

Bretons and Swiss know not the art
Nor Gascon skirt nor Toulousaine:
Two herring wives from the fisher's mart
Could shut them up, as could Lorraine,
Calais, or those of English strain
(Have I exhausted every name?)
Valenciennes of Picard plain;
There's none can touch the Paris dame.

Envoy

O Prince, to Paris women grant
The ribbon for this chatter game;
No matter how Italians rant,
There's none can touch the Paris dame.

BALLADE OF FAT MARGOT

Se j'ayme et sers la belle de bon hait

If I serve beauty to your taste,
Must I be thought a fool or knave?
Her wares are pleasing, if not chaste.
Her love can claim my sword and stave;
When clients come I drain the cave
And serve the wine without much show,
Cheese, bread, and fruit; and waters flow.
If they pay well, I say: 'Stay late;
Come back when you would rutting go,
In this brothel where we keep our state!'

But then she raves like filthy sluts
When cash is lacking in the pot;
I shun her sight, I hate her guts,
I strip her clothes and take the lot
And swear I'll sell them all for scot.
She's Antichrist; with hands on thighs
On Jesus Christ she swears and cries
That she'll not bed. I crack her pate
And bruise her well above the eyes;
In this brothel where we keep our state.

Then peace is made; I let a fart,
More bloated than a poisoned slug.
She taps my crown a playful smart,
And gives my rising flesh a hug;
Both drunk, like shoes upon a rug
We sleep. And when desires torment,
She mounts me lest my fruit be spent.
Crushed flat, I groan beneath her weight;
To slake my thirst her wiles are bent,
In this brothel where we keep our state.

La groſſe margot

FAT MARGOT
—Villon, *Le Grant Testament*
(1489)

Envoy

Come wind or hail, my bread is done.
A harlot and a leching son,
The one is with the other spun.
Bad rat, bad cat; of equal rate.
Who worship filth, it hangs upon;
And honour flies who honour shun,
In this brothel where we keep our state.

BALLADE OF SOUND ADVICE

Car ou soies porteur de bulles

For hawk you papal bulls abroad,
Or cog the dice and chance your play,
Strike monies false and then defraud,
Or roast and in the flames decay,
Like those forsworn who faith betray;
By pillage, thieving, fill the pot:
Whose is the purchase, whose the pay?
Taverns and wenches take the lot.

You rhyme and rail and strum the lute,
Like shameless mummer, foolish clown;
Or masquerade and pipe the flute;
Or play in city, village, town,
Moralities of some renown;
At skittles win, at gleek or scot:
Now listen! when the stakes are down,
Taverns and wenches take the lot.

Refrain from plying trades so coarse,
Labour and harrow, plow the tare,
Curry the mule and shoe the horse,
If lettered lines no living bear;
You'll have enough by taking care.
But scutch the hemp or tie the knot,
Be wary how you split your share:
Taverns and wenches take the lot.

Envoy

Doublets tagged and silken hose,
Whatever robes you may have got,
Before the threaded lining shows,
Taverns and wenches take the lot.

◄§ 26 §►

BALLADE OF MERCY

A *Chartreux et a Celestins*

Carthusian and Celestine monk,
Mendicant Friars, Brides of God,
Prodigal, castanetting drunk,
Servants, and wench with teasing nod
Whose coat is, like her living, odd,
Gullible fop in shameless thrall
Of love, in yellow buskin shod,
I cry your mercy, one and all.

Trollops displaying ample breast
To ply your trade with greater gain,
And thieves who after quarrels quest,
Showmen with marmots in their train,
Farceurs and fools who know chicane
And whistle six by six their call,
And boys and girls I'll not disdain,
I cry your mercy one and all.

As for that damned and traitorous hound
Who made me gnaw such bitter crust
So many days and nights around,
I think of him as dungy dust
And grant him belch and farting gust
Could I but off my bottom crawl;
At any rate, to scotch a joust,
I cry your mercy, one and all.

Envoy

May all their fifteen ribs be cracked
With heavy mallets fit to maul,
With leaded pipes and stones, in fact;
I cry your mercy, one and all.

The 'damned and traitorous hound' is Thibault d'Assigny, bishop of
Orléans, from whose prison Villon was released by the passage of Louis
XI through Meung-sur-Loire on 20 October 1461.

ANOTHER BALLADE

Icy se clost le testament

The testament is finished here
And poor Villon awaits his knell.
Come watch them sink his drafty bier
When you can hear his passing-bell;
In bright vermilion dress you well,
For Love transfixed him with his dart:
He swears it on his bagatelle,
When from this world he chose to part.

And I believe he tells no tale;
For like a scullion he was chased
About by loves in such travail
From here to Roussillon in haste
That there's no bush or brush but graced—
For once he shuns the liar's art—
With souvenirs of his shirtwaist,
When from this world he chose to part.

And thus it was he came to die
With but a rag to call his own;
What's more, Love pricked his final sigh
And turned it to a dying groan;
More piercing than was ever known
From baldric buckle was the smart
(For this was our amazement shown),
When from this world he chose to part.

Envoy

Prince like a merlin, so benign,
Hear what he did to ease his start:
He swilled a stoup of heady wine
When from this world he chose to part.

From **POÉSIES DIVERSES**

BALLADE OF GOOD COUNSEL

Hommes faillis, bersaudez de raison

You bankrupt men of twisted wit,
Unnatural, of little worth,
Devoid of sense, of reason quit,
You fools deceived, with heads of earth,
Who pile up gains against your birth,
Ignobly giving Death his head
Through cowardice! Will not this dread
Thing bite you back, become your bane?
Come see the many young bloods dead
Through taking other men's domain.

Each sees his faults and errors frail—
Seek not revenge, take it in stride;
We know this world is but a gaol:
So men of virtue, fretted, tried,
From buffets, blows, should turn aside,
At rape and murder stand aghast.
From truth divorced, by God outcast,
He taints his youth with such a stain,
And crowns his grievous traits at last
Through taking other men's domain.

To pipe and flatter, laugh and mock,
To perjure, gain without a debt,
Deceive and brew a poisoned stock,
To live in sin and sleep in sweat
From fear of neighbour—what's it get?
We sum it thus: try to atone,
Take heart, and trust in God alone;
The weeks no certain day contain;
Our parents reap the harvest sown
Through taking other men's domain.

Envoy

Seek peace, and put an end to hate;
And let accord no longer wait:
For law and the Apostle deign
To counsel Romans in this vein;
We must have order, prop, or state.
Let us take note, and tempt not fate
Through taking other men's domain.

The reference to the Apostle in the Envoy is to Romans, xii. 5: 'So we, being many, are one body in Christ, and everyone members one of another.' The Envoy has Villon's acrostic.

BALLADE OF PROVERBS

Tant grate chievre que mal gist

Goats scratch so much they spoil their bed;
Too often filled, a jug will flake;
A heated iron must turn red,
And hammered often, bend and break;
A man is worth what people take,
Gone far enough, his mind will queer,
Despised if he's sufficient rake;
Folk cry Noël until it's here.

Chatter enough, you'll contradict;
A good name's worth all grace inspired;
Too often promised, often pricked;
Pray hard enough, the thing's acquired,
The dearer it is, the more desired,
Crave it enough, you persevere,
The commoner, the less required;
Folk cry Noël until it's here.

Love dogs enough, you'll feed them well;
The shorter ditty's sooner learned;
Keep fruit too long and it will smell;
Fight hard enough, the place is earned;
The chance is lost if long adjourned,
With haste, bad luck will interfere;
From too much wooing love is spurned;
Folk cry Noël until it's here.

Excessive railing tends to tire;
A spendthrift sees his garments fray;
Be over frank, the fat's in fire;
A promise yields to 'Not today';
Who loves the Lord will often pray;
Who gives his ale must borrow beer;
A shifting wind will blow away;
Folk cry Noël until it's here.

Envoy

Prince, fools betray themselves in kind;
Who travels far must soon draw near;
The thwarted man will change his mind;
Folk cry Noël until it's here.

The refrain plays on the double meaning of the word *Noël*, a cry raised by people in medieval France in welcoming a royal progress, and *Noël*, Christmas.

BALLADE OF SMALL TALK

Je congnois bien mouches en let

I know the milk that hides a fly,
I know a man by what he wears,
I know a fair from stormy sky,
I know an orchard by its pears,
I know a tree by the sap it bears,
I know when everything's the same,
I know a drone from one who cares,
Myself I only know by name.

I know what makes a pourpoint brave,
I know a monk by his homespun,
I know a master by his knave,
I know the veil that marks a nun,
I know when pipers fool and fun,
I know fools stuffed with cream and game,
I know the vintage in the tun,
Myself I only know by name.

I know a horse, a hinny's bray,
I know their burden as a team,
I know both Beatrice and Belet,
I know what tallies up a ream,
I know a vision and a dream,
I know Bohemia's faulty claim,
I know the power of Rome supreme,
Myself I only know by name.

Envoy

Prince, briefly put, I know it all,
I know men's faces, pale, aflame,
I know well Death's consuming thrall,
Myself I only know by name.

'Bohemia's faulty claim' refers to the Hussite heresy, which had been given good publicity through the several Church councils that attempted to deal with it.

BALLADE OF UNTRUTHS

Il n'est soing que quant on a fain

Hunger alone frets years away;
Help only comes through foeman's ruse.
There's no chew like a bale of hay,
Nor vigilant watch like men who snooze;
No clemency that felons lose;
No sure man but the timorous;
Faith but in him who God eschews;
No level head not amorous.

There's breeding only in a bath;
No good repute but in exile;
No grin but from a cuff in wrath,
Nor gains but debts you reconcile.
There's no true love but fawning smile,
Nor bad luck not fortuitous;
No true report but liar's guile;
No level head not amorous.

There's no rest like a life that's tense;
No honouring but with a 'Fie!';
No vaunting but from leaden pence;
No healthy man but one awry;
No valour save what knaves belie;
No sense but from the furious;
No sweet but in a flighty eye;
No level head not amorous.

Envoy

Shall I tell you a verity?
There's no joy but in malady,
No literature but tragedy,
No coward but the chivalrous,
No grating sound but melody,
No level head not amorous.

BALLADE AGAINST THE ENEMIES OF FRANCE

Rencontré soit de bestes feu getans

May he meet with monsters belching fire
That Jason saw near the fleece of gold;
Seven years crop grass in beast's attire
As Nebuchadnezzar did of old;
Or suffer loss and bitter strife
As Trojans did for Paris' wife;
Like Tantalus be swallowed there
With Proserpine in Pluto's lair;
Or more than Job endure mischance,
With Dedalus breathe the prison air,
Who would evil wish on the realm of France!

For four months may he wail his screed
Like bittern with its tail in air;
Or to the Turk be sold for greed,
The harness of a bull to wear;
Like Magdalen spend thirty years
Without a rag to dry her tears;
Or like the drowned Narcissus lie,
Or hanged like Absalom on high,
Or as hopeless Judas was, perchance;
Or else like Simon Magus die,
Who would evil wish on the realm of France!

Return Octavian's cruel throne
To drain him of his hoarded till;
Or grind him with the floating stone
That crushed Saint Victor in the mill;
Or be swallowed in a closer spot
Than ever fell to Jonah's lot;
Or be outrun by Phoebus' pace,
Lose Venus' smile and Juno's face,
And cringe from Mars's angry glance
Like Sardanapalus in disgrace,
Who would evil wish on the realm of France!

Envoy

O Prince, by serfs whom Aeolus rules
Be snatched to Glaucus' brackish pools,
Cut off from peace and hope's last chance,
And meet the fate reserved for fools,
Who would evil wish on the realm of France!

Most of the names are those of well known biblical, mythological, or historical characters. Among the less well known are *Proserpine,* the daughter of Jupiter and Ceres who was abducted by Pluto and made queen of the underworld and mother of the Furies; *Simon Magus,* one of the founders of gnostic philosophy, is the Jewish prestidigitator who offered to buy from Saint Peter the power of working miracles (Acts, viii. 9-24)—whence our word 'simony'; *Saint Victor,* an African by birth, was pope from 185 to 197 and suffered martyrdom under Septimius Severus; *Sardanapalus* is usually identified with Ashurbanipal, a king of Assyria in the seventh century B.C. who spent the last years of his reign in riotous and voluptuous debauchery and has never lived it down; *Glaucus* is either the fisherman who was transformed into a sea-god or the unhappy man who was devoured by his horses for having defied the power of Venus.

This seems as good a place as any to say a few words about the scholarship of Master François de Montcorbier, *dit* de Villon. In the realm of the classics he shows signs of having absorbed something of Ovid, Virgil, Cato, Macrobius, Maximus, Juvenal, and Martial. To these might be added the *Organon* of Aristotle, together with the *Commentaries* of Averroes, Priscian, Porphyry's *Introduction,* Donatus, and the *Policraticus* of John of Salisbury—quite a respectable tally. He knew the Latin chronicles, the chansons de geste, the *Roman de la Rose,* and the *Liber Lamentationum* of Matheolus, and could cite with ease from ancient history and the Bible. For a fifteenth-century man, he is surprisingly well informed on contemporary affairs. Beyond all this, his M.A. degree is sufficient proof that he had got enough arithmetic, music, geometry, and astronomy to satisfy the University examiners.

BALLADE OF THE CONCOURSE OF BLOIS

Je meurs de seuf auprès de la fontaine

I die of thirst where fountains play,
With chattering teeth, like fire I burn;
In my own land I'm far away;
I shiver near a heated urn;
Nude as a grub, dressed to a turn,
I laugh through tears, despondent, wait;
Take comfort in my hopeless state;
Enjoy myself, and yet am grieved;
Am strong, and lack both strength and weight,
At once rebuffed and well received.

I'm only sure when there is doubt;
I find obscure what's evident;
When I should act, I stand about;
I keep my wits through accident;
I win, and yet am indigent;
Good Night's my usual morning quip;
Flat on my back, I fear I'll slip;
With plenty of all, of all relieved;
I'm no man's heir, but wait my ship;
At once rebuffed and well received.

With need of little, how I strain
For goods whose price I cannot pay;
Who soothes me adds but to my pain,
And tells the truth but to betray;
He is my friend who fain would say
The swan is of the raven's band;
He hurts me most who lends a hand;
Alike are truth and lies believed;
I know, but do not understand,
At once rebuffed and well received.

Envoy

Now may it please my clement Prince,
I know more than my wits evince:
Subject to every law conceived.
My wish? The pawn I've pledged long since,
At once rebuffed and well received.

Villon came to Blois in the winter of 1457, after having conveniently quit Paris following a burglary of the College of Navarre. Charles d'Orléans, one of whose seats was the château of Blois, held open house for poets after the grand manner of Eleanor of Aquitaine. Being a first-rate one himself and a person of considerable importance in the realm (leader of the Armagnac party, wounded at Agincourt, twenty-five years a prisoner of the English, father of Louis XII), he could always count on many guests. In all probability it was during one of his poetic tourneys that Villon wrote this ballade; it may even be an improvisation on a theme set by the Duke himself.

DOUBLE BALLADE

Combien que j'ay leu en ung dit

How often have I read some place:
'You judge quite wisely to beware
Of those who praise you to your face.'
Despite what people will declare,
There's no true man who does not bear
Within his heart good he betrays
Sooner or later here and there:
Requite the good with honest praise.

Saint John the Baptist did just this
When he saw God's own Lamb revealed.
In such he did not act amiss,
Exhorting crowds in open field;
So, praising God, Saint Andrew kneeled,
Knowing Him not in former days,
Yet to His Son was quick to yield:
Requite the good with honest praise.

Sweet maid from Our Lord Jesus stemmed,
Remember us poor folk below,
Poor mortals Rigour has condemned,
Who suffer Fortune's bitter blow.
From my own luck how well I know:
Through God, through you, life with me stays.
Blessèd be she who bore you so!
Requite the good with honest praise.

Here before God I now affirm
That I was like a creature dead,
But your sweet birth put off my term
In puissant charity instead,
Revived and cheered the mournful head
On which Death fixed its awful gaze;
Your presence comforts, stays my dread:
Requite the good with honest praise.

I here submit to what you will,
Reason exhorts me thus to do,
With all my poor and humble skill;
No grief is left to turn the screw,
And of annoyance, not a clue.
My life is yours—its every phase;
Both right and duty hold this true:
Requite the good with honest praise.

O grace and pity so immense,
The harbinger of utter peace,
Sum of benign benevolence,
Who from our errors grant release,
Should my encomium decrease,
Ingratitude would in me blaze,
So this refrain must never cease:
Requite the good with honest praise.

Envoy

Princess, I celebrate your fame,
I, whom from nothingness you raise.
To you, to all, I would proclaim:
Requite the good with honest praise.

This is a thank-you note to the Princess Marie d'Orléans, daughter
of Duke Charles. Villon had celebrated her birth at Blois in 1457. Now,
three years later, the child was making her first entry into her father's
capital. The largesse exhibited on this occasion saved Villon's neck, for
he was lying in the prison of Orléans under sentence of death. The
stories of Saint John and Saint Andrew (stanza ii) are told in John, i.

EPISTLE TO HIS FRIENDS

Aiez pitié, aiez pitié de moy

Good friends, have pity on my soul,
At least, if such your pleasure be!
Not holly or May tree, but this hole
Was for an exile given me
By Heaven's will and Fortune's glee.
Wenches and lovers new and old,
Leapers who dance the Calf of Gold
Swift as a dart and sharp as spear,
Gullets as clear as a mule-bell tolled,
Your poor Villon—you leave him here?

Chanters who sing as tastes demand
And laughing gallants, hail-well-met,
You ramblers free of contraband,
And nimble wits, somewhat upset,
Delay too long, Death wins the bet.
Rhymers of round, motet, and lay,
When he is dead, you'll toast the day!
He lies where breeze nor light can peer:
A stony blindfold blocks their way.
Your poor Villon—you leave him here?

Come see him in this sorry plight,
You sires from tenths and quarters quit,
By king nor emperor dubbed knight,
But holding by the Lord's own writ:
For hunger gnaws his stomach's pit;
His teeth are longer than a rake's;
After a hardened crust, not cakes,
Plain water floods his guts out clear;
No tables, beds to ease his aches.
Your poor Villon—you leave him here?

Envoy

Aforesaid Princes, old and new,
Graces and royal seals I sue,
Deliverance by basket-gear.
Even a pig will by its hue
And cry give another pig its due.
Your poor Villon—you leave him here?

The opening of this ballade is an echo of Job, xix. 21: 'Have pity upon me, have pity upon me, O ye my friends; for the hand of God hath touched me.'

REQUEST TO MONSEIGNEUR DE BOURBON

Le mien seigneur et prince redoubté

Milord and most redoubted prince,
Sired of the royal fleur-de-lys,
François Villon, whom Luck long since
Beat down with cudgels cap-a-pie,
By humble letter sends a plea
That you'll make him some gracious loan,
Which he in any court will own.
Doubt not that you'll be well content:
No interest missed, no damage shown,
You'll only lose what time is spent.

Your humble servant has no score
With others for a sou in trust.
The eighteen pounds you lent before
Have gone for food, and not for lust.
I'll pay it all at once—that's just—
But still without the least delay;
If in the forest round Patay
Acorns and chestnuts yield a rent,
I'll get your money right away:
You'll only lose what time is spent.

If I could even sell my health
To a Lombard sharper, natural leech,
I'm so caught up by lack of wealth,
Believe me, I would risk the breach.
An empty belt and shirt in reach;
Good God! how great is my surprise
That crosses never meet my eyes
Save those to which my knee is bent;
But should the real thing ever rise,
You'll only lose what time is spent.

Envoy

Prince of the lily, ever kind,
Do you know how distraught my mind
Can be if thwarted in intent?
Hear me; be favourably inclined:
You'll only lose what time is spent.

On the back of the letter

Go, letters, do a bounding jump;
Although you have no feet or tongue,
Remonstrate with resounding thump
How being broke leaves me unstrung.

Jean II, duc de Bourbon, was only three years older than Villon. Being a friend of Charles d'Orléans and a dabbler in poetry himself, he was the logical person to touch for a loan; being also a dilettante, he probably came through with the cash after reading this dunning ballade. The 'real' crosses in the third stanza refer to crosses on the reverse of coins. This sacrilegious quip was particularly daring in view of the known devotion of Louis XI to the cross of Saint-Lô.

THE HEART AND THE BODY
—G. Reisch, *Margarita Philosophica*
(1540)

THE DEBATE BETWEEN THE HEART AND THE BODY OF VILLON

Qu'est ce que j'oy? —Ce suis je! —Qui? —Ton cuer

Who's that?
　　　　—It's I!
　　　　　　　—And you?
　　　　　　　　　　—Your heart,
Which holds by but a slender strain,
No longer having force nor part
When I perceive you skulk in pain
Like some poor cur who feels the cane.
—And why?
　　　　　　—For all your stupid joy.
—What's that to you?
　　　　　　　　—A great annoy.
—Leave me!
　　　　　　—And why?
　　　　　　　　　—I shall refrain.
—And when?
　　　　　　—When I'm no longer boy.
—I speak no more.
　　　　　　　—And I'll abstain.

You think?
　　　　　—To be of eminence.
—The age of thirty, mules attain;
You call this childhood?
　　　　　　　　—No.
　　　　　　　　　　—Nonsense
Has seized you?
　　　　　　—By the neck?
　　　　　　　　　　—Inane
Your mind.
　　　　—It's not.
　　　　　　　　—What?
　　　　　　　　　—Milk with stain

Of flies I know; one's black, one's white.
—That's all?
              —*What else must I recite?*
If not enough, I'll start again.
—You're lost!
              —*I'll put up bitter fight.*
—I speak no more.
                    —*And I'll abstain.*

Mine is the grief; and yours, the ill.
Were you a fool and half insane,
Then could you plead your cause with skill:
Make no distinction, all's in vain.
Either your head's a stony brain
Or shame has honour's preference!
Then what about this consequence?
—*When I am done, where's then the stain?*
—What comfort, Lord!
                    —*What eloquence!*
—I speak no more.
                    —*And I'll abstain.*

Whence comes this ill?
                    —*From my bad luck.*
When Saturn granted me this bane
I think he must have run amuck.
—You are his lord, and not his thegn,
For Solomon scribed it in this vein:
'The wise man need not fall a prey
To orbs and planets and their sway.'
—*What they have made me, I'll remain.*
—What's that?
              —*What I believe, I say.*
—I speak no more.
                    —*And I'll abstain.*

Envoy

You want to live?
> —*May God attend!*

—Then you must . . .
> —*What?*
>> —Must make amend.

Read well.
> —*In what?*
>> —To comprehend.

Put rakes aside!
> —*That, I'll retain.*

—Now don't forget!
> —*To that I'll tend.*

—Great expectations, bitter end.

I speak no more.
> —*And I'll abstain.*

The allusion to Solomon is a quotation from the *Book of Wisdom,* vii. 19: 'Ipse enim dedit mihi horum, quae sunt, scientiam veram: ut sciam dispositionem orbis terrarum, et virtutes elementorum . . . anni cursus, et stellarum dispositionem. (For he hath given unto me true knowledge of the hours which be: that I may know the disposition of the lands of the earth, and the powers of the elements . . . the course of the year, and the disposition of the stars.)'

BALLADE TO THE NAME OF FORTUNE

Fortune fus par clers jadis nommee

Clerks gave to Fortune her good name,
By you of murder now accused,
And you a man of little fame.
Like plaster were your betters used
By poverty, and fled abused.
You've tasted shame, and you must groan?
You shouldn't; you are not alone.
Reflect upon my former deeds,
The valiant men as stiff as reeds;
Compared with them, you're but a knave.
Subside, and cease your many screeds.
Resign yourself, Villon; be brave!

Against great kings my wrath was most
Expended time now out of mind:
Priam I killed, and all his host,
What use to him was tower or blind?
Did Hannibal lag far behind?
Death there in Carthage won the cast;
And Scipio snuffed out at last;
Caesar I sold to the Senate's will;
Pompey is lost in Egypt still;
And Jason drowned beneath the wave;
And Romans burnt on every hill.
Resign yourself, Villon; be brave!

And Alexander, man of parts,
Who wished to see the Pleiades,
Was poisoned through my wily arts;
Beneath his banners in the breeze,
Arphaxad, kicked to death. I please
To do things thus, nor will I pause:
Nor need I furnish better cause.
And Holofernes, heathen wight

Whom Judith slew (he slept that night)
With his own sword—could idols save?
And Absalom? was hanged in flight.
Resign yourself, Villon; be brave!

Envoy

Then, François, heed this warning verse:
Whatever you get despite God's curse,
Naught but a rag will share your grave:
I'll make your bad luck ten times worse.
Resign yourself, Villon; be brave!

The following may not be as familiar as the other names in this ballade: *Scipio* the Younger, responsible for the destruction of Carthage in 146 B.C., was assasinated allegedly as a result of his opposition to the agrarian laws proposed by the Gracchi; the 'Romans burnt on every hill' is an allusion to Nero's fiddling; the stories of *Arphaxad*, king of the Medes, and of *Holofernes*, Nebuchadnezzar's general, are told in the book of Judith.

VILLON'S EPITAPH

Freres humains qui après nous vivez

Brothers who after us shall live,
Look not on us with scornful hate,
For if to us poor men you give
Your pity, God will mitigate
Your sins. We swing here like a gate:
The flesh we nourished well of late
Is torn to shreds, in rotten state.
And we, our bones, are dust and gall.
Let no man mock our evil fate;
But pray God He absolve us all!

Then, brothers, if we cry to you,
Disdain us not, though we be bled
To death by law. For it is true
That wit dwells not in every head;
So pardon us, since we are sped
Towards Him from Virgin Mary bred.
Let not His grace be sparing shed,
Preserve us from the devil's pall.
For we are dead: vex not the dead;
But pray God He absolve us all!

The rain has whipped and washed us white,
The sun has dried and baked and seared;
Magpies and ravens rob our sight,
Pluck out the eyebrow and the beard.
Forever upright we are geared;
First here, then there, in rhythm weird
By every gust and whirlwind steered,
More pecked than any thimble-ball.
Try not where we have persevered;
But pray God He absolve us all!

Envoy

Prince Jesus, lord of every man,
Keep us from hell's appalling ban:
We would escape that dreadful call.
Contemn not, men, our dismal·clan;
But pray God He absolve us all!

REQUEST TO THE COURT OF PARLEMENT

Tous mes cinq sens: yeulx, oreilles et bouche

All my five senses: eyes and nose,
Ears, mouth, and you, my feeling, too;
My censured members in their throes,
Speak out as you are wont to do:
'Chief Court, who set this rendezvous,
You've saved us all from sacrifice.
This tongue alone will not suffice
To praise enough and state our case;
Let all, then, speak and be precise,
Sister of angels, dame of grace!'

Weep, heart, or transfixed by a stock,
At least you might no harder be
Than that strong, greyish, desert rock
Which softened Jews by its decree:
Shed tears and make a thankful plea;
Show, humble heart, your tender side,
Extol the Court, the Empire's bride,
The Frenchman's joy, the stranger's brace,
By heaven begot and glorified,
Sister of angels, dame of grace!

Each one of you, my teeth, shake well;
Spout out your thanks and gratitude
Louder than organ, horn, or bell,
Let eating fall in desuetude;
Consider how close death pursued
And chilled my lungs, my spleen, my bile;
And you, my body, like a pile
Of mud for pigs, than bears more base,
Extol the Court, grow no more vile,
Sister of angels, dame of grace!

Envoy

Prince, but three days you'll not deny
For my appeal and my good-bye;
My cash is in another place.
Fiat, triumphant Court, my cry,
Sister of angels, dame of grace!

BALLADE OF APPEAL
Que vous semble de mon appel

What do you think of my appeal,
Garnier? Was I mad or wise?
Even a beast will watch his weal;
To shake the trap and thong he tries
Whatever means his wits devise.
Then since this homiletic quip
Was sung to me to my surprise,
Was that the time to shut my lip?

Had Hugh Capet been my forebear,
Though sprung from butcher's stock, they say,
Think for a moment they would dare
To make me drink through cloth today?
You comprehend the gentle spray?
But when this arbitrary whip
Was used in such a tricky way,
Was that the time to shut my lip?

Do you believe I lacked the zeal
And common sense enough to cry
And yell a booming: 'I'll appeal'?
Had I lacked those, I certify,
On what, I ask, could I rely?
With notary in legal scrip
About to scrawl, 'We'll hang you high!'
Was that the time to shut my lip?

Envoy

Prince I would follow Clotaire's feet
If I had suffered from the pip,
Stuck upright like a blade of wheat.
Was that the time to shut my lip?

Etienne Garnier was clerk of the Guichet at the Châtelet. The legend
that *Hugh Capet* was sprung from a family of butchers has no founda-

tion in history. The 'drink through cloth' and the 'gentle spray' are allusions to the medieval water torture known as the Question, which Wyndham Lewis describes thus: 'The stubborn one was bound, hand and foot, to staples in such a manner as to stretch his body as far as possible: a rack or trestle two feet high was placed under him, supporting his middle. The Questioner, with his assistant, then proceeded, the one to hold the prisoner's nose and thus compel him to swallow, the other to place over his mouth a horn funnel. Into this water was poured, generally four *coquemars* or pipkins-full, about nine litres altogether, by degrees, sometimes through a linen cloth. The patient was then unbound and allowed to recuperate before the treatment was (if adjudged necessary) repeated.'

ATTRIBUTED TO VILLON

ROUSING BALLADE OF THE TAVERNERS
(Attributed to Villon)

D'ung gect de dart, d'une lance asseree

By stroke of dart, by sharpened spear,
By halbert swipe and cudgel cracks,
By arrow prick and lance-hook smear,
By double sword and well-ground axe,
By two-edged tuck and dagger hacks,
By mighty snickers and a goad,
By brigands lurking on the road,
May they be butchered, cut to bits,
Their hearts torn out and stuck on spits,
Their necks lopped off with steely twine,
And dragged into the Stygian pits—
The taverners who water wine!

By Turkish dart and pointed sword
Be all their gullets liquefied,
And Grecian fire upon them poured,
Their brains by tempest scattered wide,
From gibbet hang their carrion hide,
And may they early die of gout;
I pray that they be fenced about
By red-hot bars in howling pain;
By ten strong hangmen flayed amain
And boiled in oil next day at nine,
By four great horses torn in twain—
The taverners who water wine!

Blow off their heads with cannon-ball,
And struck by thunder in the street
Let flesh and bodies of them all
Be thrown to dogs as so much meat;
And lose their sight through lightning's heat;
May snow and hail forevermore
With driving rain beat every pore,
And they without a cape or gown;
With dirks and knives slit up and down,
Drag out their corpses to the Rhine;
While eighty hammers beat their crown—
The taverners who water wine!

Envoy

Prince, may their guts be cursed on high,
Their venom terminate their line,
These traitor thieves, forsworn and sly—
The taverners who water wine!

BALLADE OF THE POOR CHIMNEY-SWEEPS
(attributed to Villon)
On parle de champs labourer

Some talk of those who plow an ell
And carry stubble in the wind,
Of those who bear a living hell
From wenches of the scolding kind;
Of monks who gnaw a bitter rind,
Of men who brave the stormy swell,
Of those who sow upon the dell
And those who have an ass in trace,
But everything considered—well,
Poor chimney-sweeps lead quite a chase!

To govern children and excel
God knows is anything but fun!
Of men-at-arms what can you tell?
Of having orders promptly done?
Of bleeding till the battle's won?
Of loving every demoiselle?
Of storming every citadel,
Of tilting at the quintain's case?
But everything considered—well,
Poor chimney-sweeps lead quite a chase!

Some think there is no parallel
To sow and reap the wheat, indeed;
To thrash and winnow out the shell,
Or come to Parlement to plead,
To borrow money when in need,
To patronize the tinker's bell,
A carter's appetite to quell,
And fast through Lent with ready grace;
But everything considered—well,
Poor chimney-sweeps lead quite a chase!

Housseur literally means a chimney-sweep, but in the argot of the regions around Amiens and Ponthieu it means quite a different kind of labourer. The Envoy is lacking.